1867 REBELLION AND CONFEDERATION

JEAN-FRANÇOIS LOZIER

CANADIAN MUSEUM OF HISTORY
MUSÉE CANADIEN DE L'HISTOIRE

Library and Archives Canada
Cataloguing in Publication

Lozier, Jean-François
1867 – Rebellion and Confederation /
Jean-François Lozier.

(Souvenir catalogue series)
Issued also in French under title:
1867 – Rébellion et Confédération.
ISBN 978-0-660-20307-2
Cat. no.: NM23-5/9-2014E

1. Canada – History – Confederation, 1867 –
Exhibitions.
2. Canada – History – 1841-1867 – Exhibitions.
3. Canada – History – 19th century –
Exhibitions.
I. Canadian Museum of History.
II. Title.
III. Series: Souvenir catalogue series.

FC161 L69 2014
971.04'9074
C2014-980048-7

Published by the
Canadian Museum of History
100 Laurier Street
Gatineau, QC K1A 0M8
www.historymuseum.ca

Printed and bound in Canada.

This work is a souvenir of the exhibition
1867 – Rebellion and Confederation,
which was developed by the Canadian
Museum of History.

Cover images:
(top) *Burning of the Houses of Assembly*,
Library and Archives Canada, e011080201
(bottom) *The Fathers of Confederation*,
Canadian Museum of History, IMG2011-
0047-0025-Dm

Souvenir Catalogue series, 9
ISSN 2291-6385

"Within your own borders peace, security and prosperity prevail, and I fervently pray that... you may be endowed with such a spirit of moderation and wisdom as will cause you to render the great work of Union which has been achieved, a blessing to yourselves and your posterity, and a fresh starting point in the moral, political and material advancement of the people of Canada."

Lord Monck, Governor General,
first Speech from the Throne, November 7, 1867

The Canadian Association of Petroleum Producers (CAPP) is proud to be National Presenting Sponsor of **1867 – Rebellion and Confederation** and Official Partner of the Canadian Museum of History's celebration of the 150th anniversary of Confederation.

CAPP applauds the Canadian Museum of History and its talented experts for creating this remarkable and educational exhibition. Through **1867 – Rebellion and Confederation**, we celebrate with all Canadians and international visitors 150 years of hard work and determination, as well as the collaborative spirit that defines our great country.

We hope that this catalogue and its exhibition will continue to stimulate passionate interest in our nation's history.

TABLE OF CONTENTS

FOREWORD

1867 – Rebellion and Confederation
takes us back to the mid-19th century
and invites us to explore the origins
of Confederation and Canadian
democracy, and to reflect on their status
today. For many, the story told in this
exhibition and this catalogue will be
a revelation. It explores a pivotal time
in Canadian history, culminating in the
dawn of Confederation and the official
birth of our country.

Among other things, the exhibition
dispels the notion that Canada's
founding was an entirely peaceful
and polite affair. The prelude to
Confederation did feature cooperation,
negotiation and compromise — those
great Canadian virtues. But our journey
to nationhood was also marred by
rebellion and riots, arson and acrimony,
hangings and deportations. The
exhibition also highlights the fact that

women, First Peoples and the landless
were disenfranchised throughout this
process of nation-building. But above
all, the exhibition, and this catalogue,
help us appreciate the remarkable
confluence of events — political, social,
economic and cultural — that gave rise
to that particular form of union at that
particular moment in history. It is, in all
respects, a fascinating story.

The year 1867 was a dramatic turning
point in Canadian history, witnessing the
dawn of Confederation and the official
birth of our country. The exhibition
likewise comes at a turning point in
the history of our national museum.
Founded in 1856, it was recently recast
as the Canadian Museum of History,
building on the legacy of predecessors
such as the Museum of Man and the
Canadian Museum of Civilization. This
exhibition testifies to our new, central

mission: to enhance public knowledge and understanding of the people, events and experiences that shaped our country's development, define the Canadian experience, and underpin our national identity.

The history preserved and presented by our museum extends back at least 12,000 years to the arrival of the country's first inhabitants. Even in that context, Confederation stands out as a seminal event. Its importance will be underlined in 2017 when Canadians mark the 150th anniversary of our unique, expanded and enduring political union. The Canadian Museum of History will play a lead role in the national commemoration. **1867 – Rebellion and Confederation** marks the beginning of that process.

Finally, I would like to emphasize that the incredible array of 200 artifacts, artwork and documents featured in this exhibition, many of which are presented in this catalogue, were drawn from our own collections and from the collections of close to 30 other institutions in Canada, Britain and the United States. To all of them, I extend the Museum's sincerest thanks.

Mark O'Neill

President and Chief
Executive Officer

Canadian Museum
of History

INTRODUCTION

BRITISH NORTH AMERICA

The Canada proclaimed on July 1, 1867 was born of both hopes and tensions. It was the culmination of a journey marked by a growing desire for autonomy, as well as newly awakened passions.

Prior to this, the word "Canada" had applied only to areas along the St. Lawrence River and the Great Lakes — the heart of what would later become Quebec and Ontario. This, in turn, was part of a larger territory, known as "British North America" following the acquisition of French territories under the 1763 *Treaty of Paris*, and recognition of American independence in 1783. At the beginning of the 19th century, British North America was composed of six separate provinces, or colonies, from west to east: Upper Canada, Lower Canada, New Brunswick, Nova Scotia, Prince Edward Island and Newfoundland. Stretching beyond British North America to the north and west was a vast territory over which the Hudson's Bay Company enjoyed a commercial and administrative monopoly, granted by the British Crown.

Significant social, cultural, economic and political changes were modernizing and transforming the colonies, and their growing populations were becoming increasingly diverse. The established order was increasingly brought into question. More and more, colonists were demanding the right to manage their own affairs, in order to better address local needs.

In the middle of the 19th century, violence, negotiation and compromise redrew the outlines of political institutions and parliamentary democracy. First, a generation struggled for and against the principle of "responsible government," which would give colonists the ability to govern themselves. The failure of the Rebellions of 1837–1838 would not discourage reformers, who would win their struggle a decade later. Regrettably, that decisive moment in Canadian history remains relatively unknown.

Faced with new challenges and opportunities, a generation of colonial politicians would develop unprecedented avenues for mutual advancement. Their draft compromise was Confederation, the union of the colonies of British North America. Canada was born in 1867, but the work of Confederation remained ongoing. The new country enjoyed greater autonomy than before in relation to Great Britain, but its independence was far from complete. It had only four provinces. The democratic rights, symbols and values we now take for granted were not yet fully established, and would only come into being gradually over the course of the 20th century. By the same token, segments of the population whose importance is unquestioned today — namely women and Aboriginal peoples — had remained marginalized within the political framework of the 19th century.

The exhibition **1867 – Rebellion and Confederation** invites us to rediscover these years of trial-and-error, upheaval, retreats and advances that led to the birth of modern Canada. This souvenir catalogue provides an overview of the objects and images gathered to tell this story. While some are well known, others are shown here for the first time.

Newfoundland

St. John's

Prince Edward Island

Lower Canada

Charlottetown

New Brunswick

Nova Scotia

Québec

Fredericton

Halifax

Upper Canada

⊛ Colonial capital

Toronto

British North America at the dawn of the 19th century

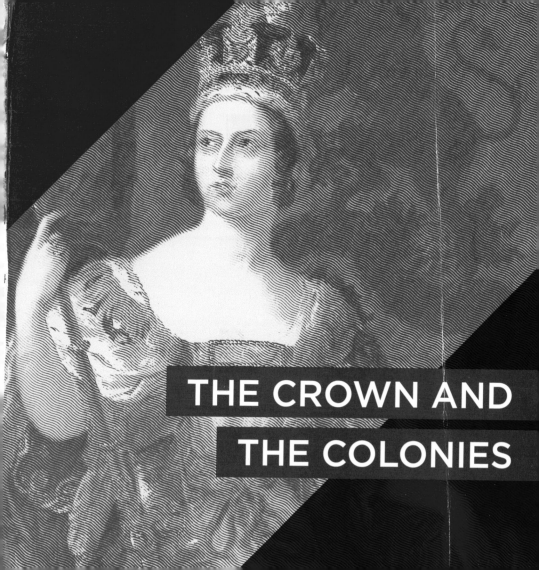

THE CROWN AND
THE COLONIES

A MONARCHY

The British North American colonies of the 19th century had inherited a government inspired by the parliamentary system of the home country. Throughout the colonies, symbols of the Crown were a constant reminder of the ties that bound them to the British Empire.

This royal coat of arms, carved in walnut, adorned the courtroom of the Court of Queen's Bench (later the Court of Appeal) in Montréal, beginning in the second half of the 19th century.

Queen Victoria ascended the throne in 1837 — following the death of her uncle, King William IV — and was crowned in great pomp and circumstance a year later. Her long reign, which extended until her own death in 1901, would come to define an era. It also coincided with the height of the British Empire, and the evolution of the British North American colonies into the young Dominion of Canada.

By the 19th century, the British monarch had long ceased to exercise absolute political power. Part of Queen Victoria's constitutional role involved giving royal assent to the decisions made by the Parliament at Westminster in London, including those that touched the colonies. Within the colonies themselves, the Queen and Parliament were represented by the Governor General, who was headquartered at Québec

Celebration of the coronation of Queen Victoria on the Halifax Common in 1838.
Watercolour by William H. Eagar.

City, and by lieutenant-governors in each of the other provincial capitals. These men generally exercised their authority by surrounding themselves with advisors and administrators drawn primarily from a small conservative elite.

However, since the end of the 18th century, each colony also had its own House of Assembly. Its members, elected by the people, debated bills that — if they earned majority support — were referred to the Legislative Council and the Governor.

A DEMOCRACY IN THE MAKING

During this period, more people in British North America had access to the vote than almost anywhere else in the world. Yet voting rights remained limited. Several segments of society were either formally or informally excluded, including women, Aboriginal peoples, and the poor. Ultimately, the right to vote was a privilege reserved primarily for men who were established. Voting conditions set forth by law also opened the door to a host of questionable practices. Corruption, intimidation and violence often disrupted elections and influenced their results.

The powers of the legislative assemblies were further limited because, in keeping with the colonial model, the governors and their political allies kept the exercise of power for themselves. Accountable only to the British Parliament, they could reject bills submitted by the assemblies. The will of the colonial electorate was therefore easily and frequently ignored. The government, in short, was not an elected body.

At the centre of the assembly chamber of each colony, a ceremonial mace served as a reminder that the assembly's authority was delegated by the Crown. These maces evoked an earlier time, when the Sergeant-at-Arms could be called upon to defend the monarch with physical force.

This particular mace — made of carved and painted wood, rather than precious metals — was given by British authorities to the Newfoundland House of Assembly when that House was established in 1833. It was used until 1950, when it was replaced with a mace presented by the Legislative Assembly of British Columbia, in honour of Newfoundland joining Confederation a year earlier.

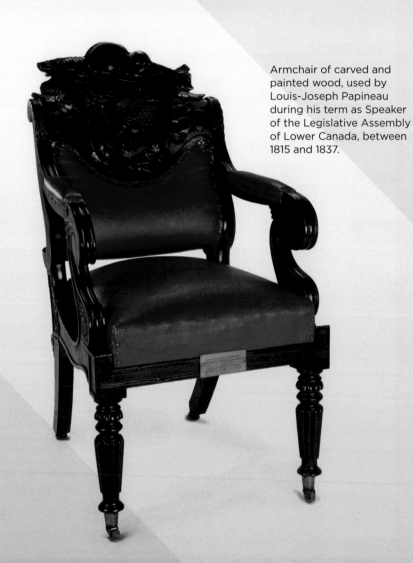

Armchair of carved and painted wood, used by Louis-Joseph Papineau during his term as Speaker of the Legislative Assembly of Lower Canada, between 1815 and 1837.

View of Province House, the seat of the Nova Scotia House of Assembly in Halifax.

Watercolour by John Elliott Woolford, 1819.

HUNGER FOR CHANGE

Political parties as we know them today did not yet exist during this period — instead they took the form of fluid and informal interest groups. The established order benefitted from the support of those variously known as "Tories," "loyalists," or "constitutionalists," who supported a conservative political philosophy. On the opposite side, other segments of the colonial population, inspired by the democratic and anticolonial movements that were rocking Europe and the Americas, demanded reforms. They described themselves as "reformers," "liberals," "radicals," and sometimes "republicans," and, in Lower Canada, "Patriotes."

In each colony, reformers aggressively denounced the authoritarianism of the existing government. In Lower Canada in 1834, Louis-Joseph Papineau and members of the Patriote Party submitted a series of 92 resolutions demanding a responsible and representative government, elected by the people of the colonies. The Colonial Secretary in London, Lord Russell, utterly rejected their demands. The petitions of reformers in Upper Canada and Nova Scotia — directed by William Lyon Mackenzie and Joseph Howe, respectively — were similarly brushed aside.

Leaders of the reform movement in Lower Canada during the 1830s, left to right: Edmund Bailey O'Callaghan, Louis-Joseph Papineau, Denis-Benjamin Viger, Wolfred Nelson. The figure on the right, identified as "Montfeiraud" (sic), is none other than the celebrated Jos Montferrand or Joe Mufferaw, who lent his strength to reform candidates during some of the more hotly contested elections.

Lithography by Alfred Ducôte after John Doyle, published in 1838.

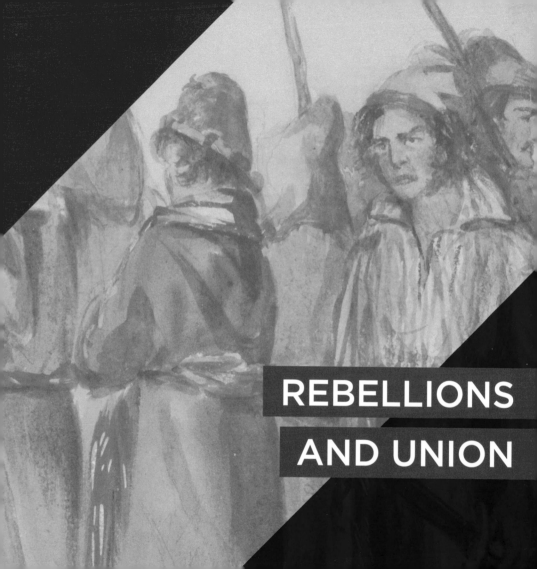

REBELLIONS AND UNION

REBELLION

In 1837, political tensions in the colonies boiled over into armed conflict. Frustrated by the rejection of their demands, reformers in Lower Canada gathered in assemblies at which they denounced the tyranny of Great Britain and challenged the authority of its representatives. More radical leaders like Louis-Joseph Papineau urged people to take up arms. The conflict began in Montréal in November, before spreading to the countryside. Rebels in Upper Canada, led by William Mackenzie, soon followed suit.

In Lower Canada, the Patriotes enjoyed significant support among farmers, day labourers and artisans in the Montréal area and the Richelieu Valley. Although primarily francophone, the movement also included a significant English and Irish minority. In Upper Canada, a large number of the rebels were farmers of American origin.

The rebels in both Upper and Lower Canada were deeply committed to their cause, but were disorganized and poorly armed. Following a brief victory at Saint-Denis-sur-Richelieu

The Insurgents of Beauharnois, 1838.
Watercolour by Katherine Jane Ellice.

in November 1837, the Patriotes of Lower Canada suffered a series of crushing defeats. In December, following skirmishes with the militia, most of the rebels of Upper and Lower Canada fled in the confusion. In 1838, insurgents with the support of American sympathizers nevertheless kept authorities on high alert. After two years of intermittent conflict, the rebels were defeated for good.

To supplement British troops, several volunteer units were recruited and equipped by prominent Tory merchants opposed to the reformers. One of these units, the Queen's Light Dragoons, was organized in Montréal at the outbreak of the rebellion. A detachment of that unit would guard Lord Elgin, the Governor, during the riots that shook the city in 1849.

Shako worn by Henry R. Williams, cavalryman in the Queen's Light Dragoons, 1837. Williams later became a grocer and postmaster in Brome County, Canada East (Quebec).

Officer of the Queen's Light Dragoons, around 1847 (right).
Lithography by G. & W. Endicott after James Cane.

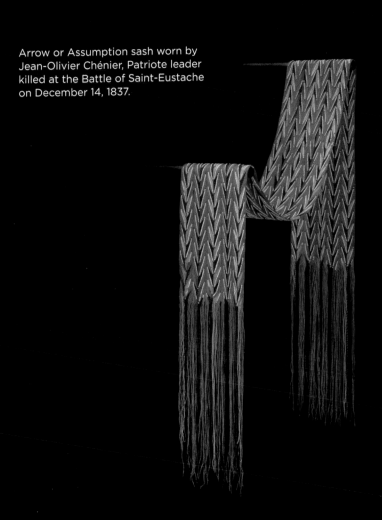

Arrow or Assumption sash worn by Jean-Olivier Chénier, Patriote leader killed at the Battle of Saint-Eustache on December 14, 1837.

Powder horn used by
Léon Quemeneur-Laflamme,
habitant and Patriote, at the Battle
of Saint-Denis-sur-Richelieu on
November 23, 1837.

Fort Henry, in Kingston, where several insurgents were imprisoned.
Watercolour by George St. Vincent, around 1840.

PRISON, EXILE AND THE GALLOWS

In Lower Canada, martial law was declared and was accompanied by particularly brutal repression. The victory of loyalist troops gave rise to a wave of looting and devastation in the countryside. Entire villages were burned to the ground.

Following these confrontations, several leaders, including Papineau and Mackenzie, took refuge in the United States. In all, nearly 1,500 people were arrested, 250 were deported to Australia and Bermuda, and 50 were hanged.

In the prisons of Upper Canada, men awaiting trial made souvenir boxes like these. Their poetic inscriptions attest to a profound feeling of injustice.

Boxes carved by L.E.D. Efton, William Reid, John Anderson (Toronto) and George Barclay, Jr. (Kingston) in 1838.

THE MISSION OF "RADICAL JACK"

In London, as in Canada, colonial authorities were shaken by the uprisings of 1837 and 1838. Lower Canada's House of Assembly, now considered too radical, was dissolved. The British government made John George Lambton, Lord Durham, Governor-in-Chief of the British North American colonies, and asked him to enquire into the origins of the Rebellions.

Lord Durham's time in the colonies lasted less than six months, but would have far-reaching consequences. Back in England, he issued a report which stressed the importance of democratic reforms, but which also constituted a serious attack on the rights of French Canadians. To restore peace and harmony, he proposed three solutions: union of the two Canadas; responsible government; and the assimilation of French Canadians, whom he considered to be "a people with no history, and no literature," with no hope of surviving in North America. The goal of the union of the two colonies was to diminish the political power of French-speaking Lower Canadians.

Oil on canvas attributed to
Sir Thomas Lawrence, around 1830.

Lord Durham, depicted in the prime of life on page 35, was a notable reformer. Although a wealthy aristocrat, he took a lively interest in the rights of the emerging middle class. The support he gave to a number of progressive causes in England — particularly economic free trade and public education — earned him the nickname "Radical Jack."

UNION OF THE CANADAS

To avoid future rebellions, and believing that a colonial assembly dominated by the British element would strengthen imperial ties, Britain's Parliament willingly implemented one of Lord Durham's recommendations, and decreed the union of Upper and Lower Canada.

The 1840 *Act of Union* created the Province of Canada, otherwise known as the United Canadas, and made English the sole official language in its Legislative Assembly. However, Great Britain rejected the idea of giving colonists the right to govern their own affairs.

Great Seal of the Province of Canada, used beginning in 1841. By law, it was defaced when a new Great Seal was issued in 1869.

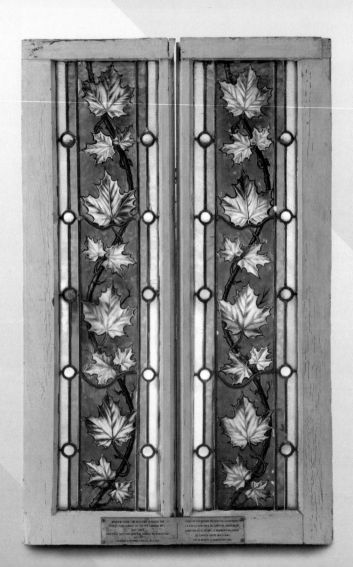

Stained-glass window from the Kingston General Hospital, dating to when the building housed the Parliament of Canada.

A NEW CAPITAL

The first Governor of the united Province of Canada, Lord Sydenham, made Kingston the capital in 1841. Parliament sat in the brand-new Kingston General Hospital building. At first glance, the Anglophone character of this central and prosperous town made it seem a suitable capital to those seeking the assimilation of French Canadians. In 1844, however, members of the Assembly decided to move the capital to Montréal, preferring that city's more dynamic and cosmopolitan character. They met in the St. Anne's Market building.

Kingston General Hospital, around 1857 (left) and Sainte-Anne's Market building, around 1839 (right).

TOWARDS RESPONSIBLE GOVERNMENT

THE WINDS OF REFORM

The failure of the Rebellions and the proclamation of the *Act of Union* made one thing clear: the British government would not be relinquishing any of its authority to the colonies. Reformers in the now-united colonies of Canada West (previously Upper Canada) and Canada East (previously Lower Canada) understood that, despite their linguistic and cultural differences, they would need to work together to advance their cause. They made responsible government — the principle according to which the government must enjoy the confidence of the majority of the members of the Legislative Assembly — their key issue. For French Canadians, another major concern was the preservation of their identity, which was now coming under threat.

Against all expectations, the *Act of Union* initiated a dialogue between moderate Anglophone and Francophone reformers. New alliances were soon formed to promote common causes.

Legislative Assembly Chamber, Montréal, around 1848.
Watercolour by James Duncan.

JOINING FORCES

Although several of the rebel leaders defeated in 1837–1838 preferred to remain in a more or less voluntary exile, including Papineau, others such as Wolfred Nelson and the young George-Étienne Cartier returned to political life with a more moderate approach. Two men, who had remained on the fringes of the armed conflict, would make a name for themselves in these years: Louis-Hippolyte La Fontaine, leader of the reformers in Canada East, and Robert Baldwin, his counterpart in Canada West.

La Fontaine and Baldwin, both of whom sought to achieve responsible government and the reform of colonial institutions, decided to join forces. In addition to developing a common political ideology, which held that parties must be founded on (political) "opinions," rather than (ethnic) "origins," they developed a deep friendship. Following La Fontaine's electoral defeat in 1841, Baldwin gave him the opportunity to stand as a candidate before sympathetic Anglophone voters in York County, in Canada West. La Fontaine returned the favour two years later, inviting Baldwin to stand as a candidate before equally sympathetic Francophone voters in the county of Rimouski, in Canada East.

Robert Baldwin, oil painting by Théophile Hamel, around 1848.

Louis-Hippolyte La Fontaine, oil painting by Théophile Hamel, around 1848.

STRUGGLE IN THE MARITIMES

The reform movement was also active in the Atlantic colonies. In Nova Scotia, publisher Joseph Howe was one of its most brilliant promoters. He never missed an opportunity to criticize abuses of power by the governing elites in the Legislative Assembly, where he sat as a member, or in his newspapers.

Howe's words often provoked great controversy. In 1835, the government prosecuted him for seditious libel. In 1840, he was challenged to a duel by John Halliburton, son of the colony's chief justice. When the day came, Halliburton shot first, but missed. The gallant Howe discharged his own weapon into the air, feeling that the honour of the reformers had been defended.

Joseph Howe, pastel by T. Debaussy, 1851.

This snuffbox was presented to James Boyle Uniacke — another leader, with Howe, of the Nova Scotia reformers — in 1844, when he refused to join the executive council as a protest against the patronage and misconduct of the colony's Lieutenant-Governor, Lord Falkland. The inscription indicates that the snuffbox was presented to Uniacke "by the friends of constitutional government in Halifax, as a token of respect for his abilities and consistent public conduct."

A QUESTION OF LOYALTY

During these years, the principle of responsible government continued to arouse strong opposition. The Tory conservative elites and their supporters, considering themselves to be the only loyal subjects, sought to protect their privileged position, and to defend their own political and economic interests.

In general, however, the reformers did not consider themselves any less loyal than their opponents. By demanding responsible government, they were not calling into question the British system and British institutions — far from it. They were only asking, they believed, for the local application of a principle long upheld in Great Britain.

To be clear, the camps were not always strongly united. Some supported reform in certain areas, while fearing that responsible government would overly weaken ties with the mother country. Allan Napier MacNab, for example, was one of the most ardent supporters of economic reform, but remained fiercely opposed to the political reforms proposed by Baldwin and La Fontaine. Egerton Ryerson, a major advocate of reform when it came to public education and a tireless critic of abuses of power, was opposed to the principle of responsible government, considering it both overly radical and too premature.

This rare banner was displayed by supporters of John Henry Dunn and Isaac Buchanan in 1842. To everyone's surprise, these two reform candidates, allies of Baldwin, had both won seats in Toronto during the previous year's elections. Humiliated by their defeat, the Tories sparked a riot, during which a supporter of Dunn and Buchanan was killed. In the end, the decade's political moderation was only relative.

A TURNING POINT

The governors sent to the colony during these years were mandated, first and foremost, to uphold the prerogatives of the Crown, and to resist the development of responsible government. Some made concessions on certain points: Lord Metcalfe, Governor General from 1843 to 1845, distanced himself from the idea of assimilating the French population. Still, antagonism persisted between governors and their allies on the one hand, and reformers on the other.

The political tide was turning in Great Britain. The British Parliament, motivated by new economic, political and social priorities, became more open to letting colonists manage their

Sir Charles Metcalfe at the Opening of Parliament in Montréal, 1845.
Oil on canvas by Andrew Morris.

own economic and domestic affairs. James Bruce, 8th Earl of Elgin and 12th Earl of Kincardine, better known as Lord Elgin, was made Governor of the Province of Canada in 1847, with instructions to establish responsible government.

Lord Elgin and his entourage leaving the Governor General's residence for Parliament, April 1849.

Ink drawing by Francis Augustus Grant.

BUILT TO LAST?

In early 1848, reformers under the leadership of Baldwin and La Fontaine elected more members to the Legislative Assembly of the Province of Canada than their opponents. Lord Elgin accordingly implemented the much-anticipated principle of responsible government, inviting the reformers to form the government, and agreeing to give assent to the laws they would pass.

The *Rebellion Losses Bill*, introduced by La Fontaine as Premier, proved controversial. It was intended to compensate people in Lower Canada who had incurred losses during the Rebellions. Despite the strong opposition of conservative-leaning members, who saw the measure as one that rewarded disloyal subjects, it was approved by the reformist majority that now dominated the Assembly.

Lord Elgin, as promised, gave his assent to the bill, drawing the contempt and anger of the Tories. English-language newspapers issued a call to arms. The protests, which converged on the Parliament building, degenerated into riots. Rioters first threw rocks at the building, shattering its windows, then pushed their way inside and vandalized everything in sight. They ended by setting fire to Parliament. One of the arsonists turned out to be the chief of a fire brigade.

The Burning of Parliament in Montréal, around 1849.

Oil on wood by Joseph Légaré.

The burning of Parliament in Montréal on the night of April 25, 1849, was the culmination of a decade of tension and bitterness. In the painting on pages 54-55, Joseph Légaré depicted the intensity of the fire.

The riots would continue for several days. These rocks were thrown at Lord Elgin's carriage on April 30. Lady Elgin, careful to preserve the memory of these historic events, collected the projectiles and added commemorative inscriptions

A MAJOR STEP TOWARDS DEMOCRACY

The triumph of responsible government in British North America owes much to Lord Elgin. Like Lord Durham, who was none other than his father-in-law, Elgin firmly believed in the principle of colonial autonomy. However, not sharing the assimilating prejudices of his predecessor, he welcomed French Canadians to power on an equal footing with the English. Despite the riots in Montréal, he chose to uphold the principle of responsible government, thus becoming the first Governor General to distance himself from the affairs of the Legislative Assembly, and to leave real power in the hands of elected representatives. It was an important victory for democracy. Within the space of seven years, the lieutenant-governors of the other colonies would follow his lead.

In Nova Scotia, Lieutenant-Governor Sir John Harvey had already played a role similar to that of Elgin by introducing responsible government in February 1848 — a month before Elgin did so in the Province of Canada.

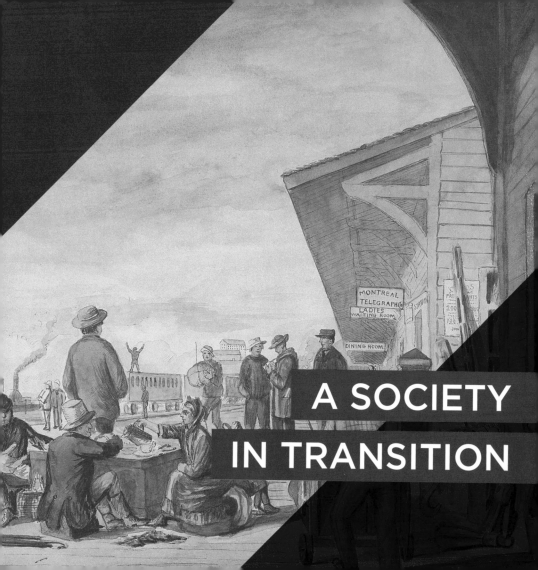

A SOCIETY
IN TRANSITION

HOPE FOR A BETTER LIFE

Immigration, which intensified during the 19th century, transformed the demographic landscape of British North America. Attracted by the availability of land, new arrivals came primarily from the British Isles. The Irish, fleeing famine, sickness and poverty — particularly following the Great Famine of 1845–1852 — came in particularly large numbers.

In addition to the British, the colonies also attracted numerous Americans and Europeans. Expanding from 95,000 inhabitants in 1815 to more than 950,000 by 1851, Upper Canada or Canada West experienced the most significant growth of the colonies. The newcomers, while retaining their culture and way of life, gradually began to merge and to adopt common symbols.

This jacket belonged to Patrick Quinn, a young Irish boy who was orphaned shortly after his arrival in 1847, at the age of 6. Adopted by a French-Canadian family, he would enjoy a lengthy career as a parish priest.

The First Union Station, Toronto, 1859. It had been built at the bottom of Yonge Street, near the harbour, the previous year.

Watercolour by William Armstrong.

PROTECTING THEIR DIFFERENCES

Despite maintaining a high birth rate, French Canadians became a minority during this period. Faced with the prospect of assimilation expressed in the *Durham Report* and the *Act of Union*, they became increasingly aware of their differences when it came to the French language and the Catholic religion.

Responding to the words of Lord Durham, who had said that French Canadians were "a people with no history, and no literature," François-Xavier Garneau, a young civil servant, wrote an early *Histoire du Canada* (History of Canada). Around the same time, the Société Saint-Jean-Baptiste was founded to defend French-Canadian interests, and the Civil Code of Lower Canada was drafted to reflect their distinct judicial heritage.

Also seeking to preserve their specific cultural and religious practices, many immigrants founded mutual aid societies based on models which existed in their countries of origin. Protestants rallied under the banner of the Loyal Orange Lodge, while Irish Catholics formed the St. Patrick's Society and the Scots established the St. Andrew's Society. These groups — particularly Catholics and Protestants — greatly distrusted one another and regularly came to blows.

Orange parade at the corner of King Street E. and Yonge Street, Toronto, around 1867.

Albumen proof.

Erected in the early 1860s, this boundary marker — bearing the old names "Upper Canada" and "Lower Canada" — reveals the ways in which old divisions persisted in the Province of Canada, despite the 1840 political union.

Brooch featuring a maple leaf, worn during the visit of the Prince of Wales to Canada in 1860.

Brooch featuring a beaver, 1847.

A UNITED CANADA?

The interests of the people and politicians in the two former halves of the united Province of Canada continued to diverge. The climate of conflict that resulted made the whole very difficult to govern. The politicians of Canada West loudly demanded "rep by pop": representation proportional to the population, which would better reflect the growth of the Anglophone population in their part of the province. The politicians of Canada East, where Francophones remained a majority, were against the proposition, as it threatened to stifle their voice, their interests, and their identity.

And yet, the population was developing a common identity. The maple leaf and the beaver had long been national symbols among French Canadians. As British colonists developed a stronger attachment to their new home, they too adopted these emblems, beginning in the 1840s. They similarly adopted the word "Canadian," which had previously been used only by the Francophone population. Only later would the people of the Atlantic colonies eventually come to share this name and these emblems.

AN EXPANDING ECONOMY

The economy of the British North American colonies was expanding in the mid-19th century. For the most part, it remained dependent on natural resources, but the primary sector diversified and intensified. Resources such as lumber, wheat, fish and coal, as well as furs, were intended mainly for export — to Great Britain, the British colonies in the West Indies and, increasingly, to the United States.

At the same time, advances in technology and means of production sparked significant economic and social change in the colonies. Industrialization appeared first in the Province of Canada, in cities such as Montréal and Toronto, where access to a female, child and immigrant workforce kept production costs down. The first sectors to be affected were food-processing, clothing, footwear and tobacco. Manufactured goods gradually began to replace handcrafted items.

The arrival of the industrial era in the colonies led to explosive growth in the transportation and communications sectors. The movement of people, goods and ideas accelerated. In the colonies, the first railway was launched in 1836, and reliable transatlantic steam travel was established by 1840. Canals, such as Lachine and Welland, increased in number to facilitate navigation throughout the interior. The colonies' first telegraph company — the Toronto, Hamilton and Niagara Electro-Magnetic Telegraph Company — was launched in 1846.

The financial sector evolved in tandem with industrialization. A number of businessmen, who had grown rich through the trade in lumber and wheat, enjoyed an extended network of contacts in Great Britain and the United States, and monitored foreign industrial developments closely. They invested heavily in the building of factories, and made significant profits from the sale and transportation of manufactured goods. To protect their customers' savings and to finance their own ventures, they founded dozens of banks.

The people in the colonies — particularly those in Canada West — had become increasingly interested in the West by the mid-19th century. Settlers and businessmen had their eye on that vast region, over which the Hudson's Bay Company still enjoyed a monopoly. Such ambitions took little notice of the Aboriginal peoples who already occupied the land. Fledgling colonies, like the one on Vancouver Island, founded in 1848, paved the way for the European settlement of Canada. The railway promised to link the colonies, from sea to sea.

Rolling mills in Toronto, where steel rails were produced to meet the needs of expanding railway networks.
Pastel by William Armstrong, 1864.

THE AMERICAN PROMISE AND THREAT

During the 19th century, the United States represented both promise and a threat to British North America. The peace between the colonies of British North America and the young republic was precarious. During the Rebellions of 1837–1838, American sympathizers attempted to come to the aid of rebels by launching raids on Upper and Lower Canada. Around the same time, the ill-defined border between Maine, Lower Canada and New Brunswick became a source of tension. In 1842, the signing of the Webster-Ashburton Treaty averted armed conflict, but the inhabitants of the colonies would continue distrusting American intentions for many years to come.

The American economy, on the other hand, exerted a pull that was difficult to resist. The people of British North America had contradictory attitudes towards their American neighbour. While some feared political union with the United States, others saw only the promise of democracy and economic prosperity. A short-lived movement advocating annexation arose in 1849. In 1854, a Reciprocity Treaty introduced a form of free trade and created new American outlets for colonial products. This new economic openness silenced most Canadian advocates of annexation.

Long dependent on trade with Great Britain and the United States, British North America was vulnerable to foreign economic crises. In 1865, when the United States announced the end of the Reciprocity Treaty, new solutions had to be found. Some businessmen and politicians saw the advantages of an east-west trade, which could be fostered by improved railway links. British financiers, some of whom came together under the banner of the British North America Association, expressed an interest in investing in major colonial projects.

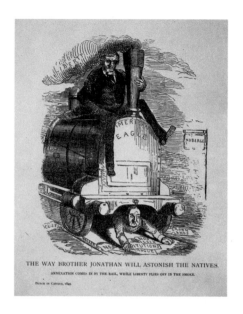

THE WAY BROTHER JONATHAN WILL ASTONISH THE NATIVES.

ANNEXATION COMES IN BY THE RAIL, WHILE LIBERTY FLIES OFF IN THE SMOKE.

PUNCH IN CANADA, 1849.

"Brother Jonathan," the predecessor of Uncle Sam, crushes a poor Canadian with his annexation locomotive.

Political cartoon by John Henry Walker, published in the magazine *Punch in Canada* in 1849.

AN INVASION?

The democratic spirit that drove the young American republic filled many reformers in the British colonies with admiration, but its aggressive and populist nature also gave rise to distrust and fear. Many public figures in the United States expressed a desire to annex the British colonies — by force, if necessary.

Having long viewed the North American colonies as a bastion of the Empire, Great Britain now began to see them as an economic burden that was virtually impossible to defend in military terms. Many British politicians felt that, since the colonies now enjoyed responsible government, they should also take on financial responsibility for major projects such as the railway — and, of course, the defence of their own borders.

An invasion was anticipated. The American Civil War (1861–1865), a conflict between the American federal government and the Confederate southern states, who sought greater political autonomy and defended the institution of slavery, was viewed with profound ambivalence in the British colonies. Great Britain and its colonies profited from trade with the southern states and sympathized with them, despite the fact that the abolition of slavery was a popular cause here. This show of sympathy led to a number of incidents: British ships were illegally

In this political cartoon, "Ce bon Monsieur Lincoln" (The good Mr. Lincoln), seated behind an army encampment, spies covetously on Canada, while the British garrison prepares ramparts for an anticipated assault. Above the ramparts, an archetypal Canadian figure thumbs his nose at the American leader.

Political cartoon by Charles-Henri Moreau, published in the newspaper *Le Perroquet*, April 15, 1865.

boarded and searched at sea by American ships; and Confederate raiders took refuge in Canada after robbing a series of banks in the state of Vermont. It was feared that the war might spread northward.

As soon as the Civil War came to an end, a new threat emerged: that of the Fenian Brotherhood, an association seeking to free Ireland from the British yoke. To achieve their ends, the Fenians hoped to take the North American colonies hostage via the United States. In 1866, they attempted to invade Campobello Island in New Brunswick, as well as Canada from the border at Niagara. Although their means did not match their ambitions, they caused considerable disruption and aroused significant apprehension in the colonies.

The Fenians included several soldiers discharged after the American Civil War. This kepi was worn by one of these veterans. The revolver was confiscated on June 2, 1866 from a Fenian officer at Limeridge, near Ridgeway in Canada West (Ontario).

Kepi, 1866–1870.
Revolver, 1856–1866.

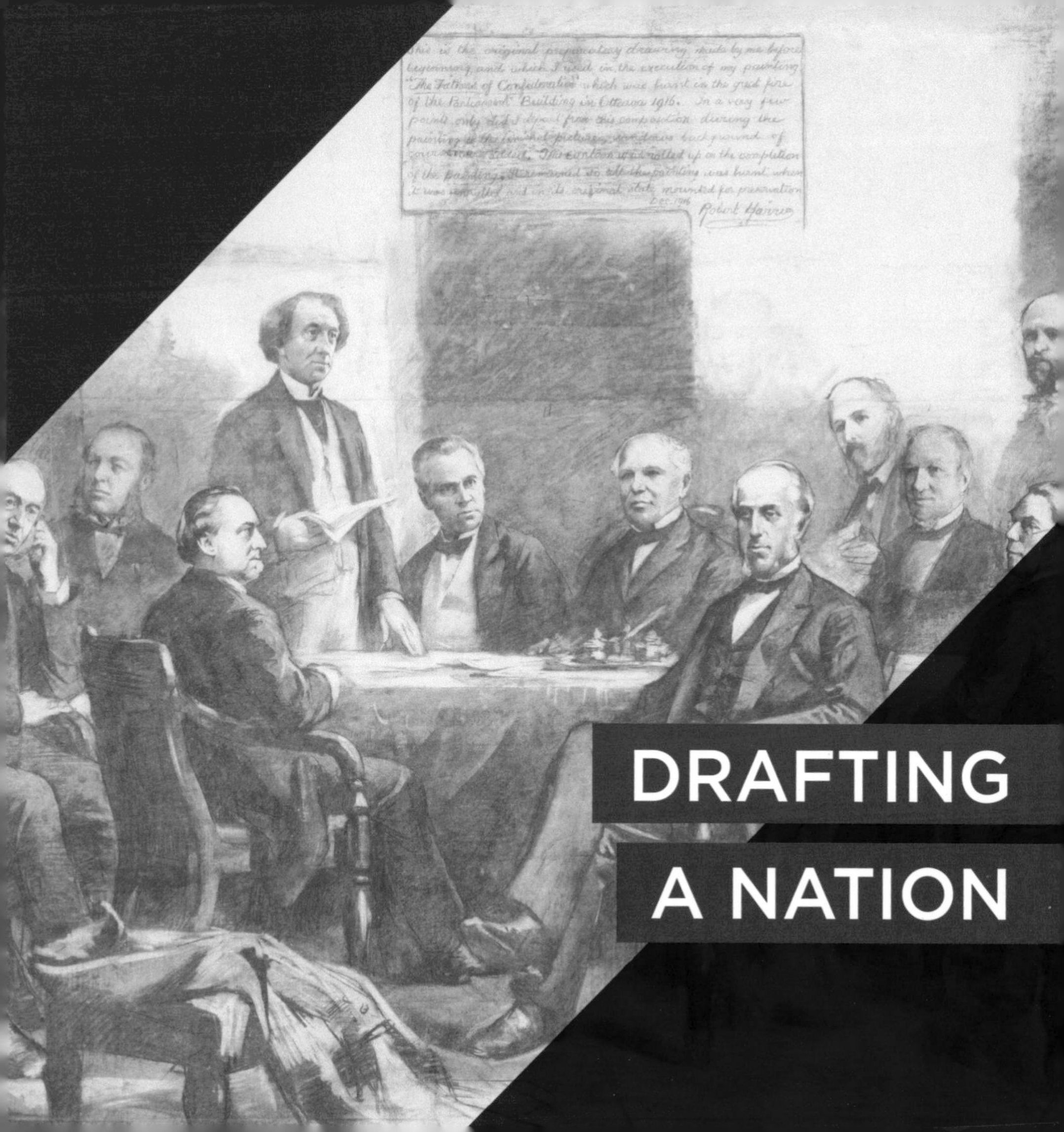

DRAFTING A NATION

TOWARDS A BROADER UNION

British North America had undergone profound transformations within the space of a quarter-century. In the early 1860s, it faced new social, political and economic realities. The political structures established by the *Act of Union* were no longer enough. Tensions were rising. French Canadians, far from having been assimilated, had stood up for their rights. Their compatriots of British origin, now a majority in Canada West, demanded greater autonomy. In United Canada, no fewer than six governments fell in as many years. In the meantime, markets were struggling, and economic growth was in jeopardy. To the south, the Americans were more menacing than ever. An impasse had been reached.

In the minds of some politicians, there was a solution to the various problems that plagued the colonies: the unification of all of British North America. This was not a new idea — Lord Durham had raised the possibility in his 1839 Report — but the idea of a "great confederation" gained new momentum around 1860.

The year 1864 would be a turning point. Political leaders in the Province of Canada, led by John A. Macdonald, George-Étienne Cartier and George Brown, took the initiative. Setting aside their political differences, they formed a "Great Coalition" with the specific objective of carrying out this project.

This illustration, published in the *Canadian Illustrated News* on May 23, 1863, depicts an event that had become routine in United Canada in these years: the fall of a government — in this case that of the moderate Liberal, John Sandfield Macdonald.

Macdonald, Cartier and Brown, photographed by Notman in Montréal, in 1862–1863.

THE *SS QUEEN VICTORIA*

Canadian delegates set sail for Charlottetown in 1864, aboard the *SS Queen Victoria*. This steam-powered sailing ship normally carried out coastguard duties for the Canadian government, but was sometimes used for official functions. It occasionally transported the Governor General, and in 1860 it brought the Prince of Wales to visit the country. During the Charlottetown Conference, it served as the headquarters for Macdonald, Cartier and Brown.

Anonymous painting of the *SS Napoleon III*, sister ship to the *SS Queen Victoria*, around 1856.

THE CONFEDERATION BELL

This bell, which graced the bridge of the *SS Queen Victoria*, sounded in the port of Charlottetown at the end of the summer of 1864. Chartered two years later to pick up a cargo of fruit in Cuba, the ship was caught in a hurricane and sank. The crew was rescued by the *Ponvert*, a sailing ship out of Prospect Harbor, Maine. The grateful Canadian captain offered his American counterpart his own ship's bell and silverware.

CHARLOTTETOWN: SPECIAL GUESTS

At the end of the summer of 1864, delegates from Nova Scotia, New Brunswick and Prince Edward Island gathered in Charlottetown to discuss a possible union of the Maritime colonies.

The Canadian delegation — led by John A. Macdonald, George-Étienne Cartier and George Brown — invited itself to their meeting. Taking advantage of the working sessions, as well as the related banquets and balls, the Canadian delegates did their best to convince their counterparts of the benefits of a broader union, and debated with them the main points of their initiative.

Province House, Charlottetown, seat of the Legislative Assembly of Prince Edward Island and location of the Charlottetown Conference.

Image from the *Illustrated London News*, November 12, 1864.

Delegates to the Charlottetown Conference, 1864.
Photograph by George P. Roberts.

BALLS AND BANQUETS

Beyond the official sessions of the Conference, a host of social activities allowed delegates to get to know one another while sharing the dream of a common country. The Lieutenant-Governor and other Prince Edward Island notables held a dinner and a grand ball in the delegates' honour. The Canadians returned the favour by giving a banquet aboard the SS *Queen Victoria*, where the champagne flowed freely. "Whether as the result of our eloquence or of the goodness of our champagne," wrote George Brown to his wife Ann, "the ice became completely broken."

WOMEN IN THE SHADOWS

Women had long been kept on the political sidelines. At the Charlottetown, Quebec and London Conferences, however, many delegates were accompanied by their wives and daughters. These women played a major role, helping to break the ice during society balls and banquets.

Mercy Ann Coles, who accompanied her father from Charlottetown to Québec City, carefully recorded her impressions of the events in her diary.

Mercy Ann Coles in 1864.
Photograph by William Notman.

A MEETING IN QUÉBEC CITY

Having come to an agreement on the principle of a colonial union, the delegates decided to further the discussion in Québec City. In October 1864, they met in the library of the Canadian Parliament building to debate two major visions: one favouring a strong central government; the other upholding provincial autonomy.

Parliament Building for the Province of Canada, site of the Quebec Conference, around 1860.

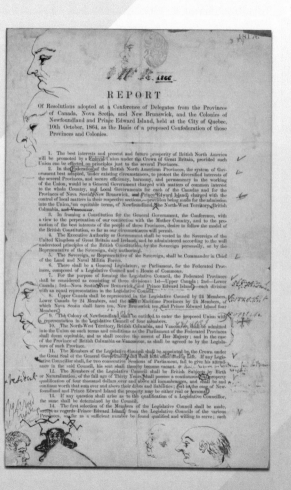

REPORT

Of Resolutions adopted at a Conference of Delegates from the Provinces of Canada, Nova Scotia, and New Brunswick, and the Colonies of Newfoundland and Prince Edward Island, held at the City of Quebec, 10th October, 1864, as the Basis of a proposed Confederation of those Provinces and Colonies.

1. The best interests and present and future prosperity of British North America will be promoted by a Federal Union under the Crown of Great Britain, provided such Union can be effected on principles just to the several Provinces.

2. In the Federation of the British North American Provinces, the system of Government best adapted, under existing circumstances, to protect the diversified interests of the several Provinces, and secure efficiency, harmony, and permanency in the working of the Union, would be a General Government charged with matters of common interest to the whole Country, and Local Governments for each of the Canadas and for the Provinces of Nova Scotia, New Brunswick, and Prince Edward Island, charged with the control of local matters in their respective sections,—provision being made for the admission into the Union, on equitable terms, of Newfoundland, the North-West Territory, British Columbia, and Vancouver.

3. In framing a Constitution for the General Government, the Conference, with a view to the perpetuation of our connection with the Mother Country, and to the promotion of the best interests of the people of these Provinces, desire to follow the model of the British Constitution, so far as our circumstances will permit.

4. The Executive Authority or Government shall be vested in the Sovereign of the United Kingdom of Great Britain and Ireland, and be administered according to the well understood principles of the British Constitution, by the Sovereign personally, or by the Representative of the Sovereign, duly authorized.

5. The Sovereign, or Representative of the Sovereign, shall be Commander in Chief of the Land and Naval Militia Forces.

6. There shall be a General Legislature, or Parliament, for the Federated Provinces, composed of a Legislative Council and a House of Commons.

7. For the purpose of forming the Legislative Council, the Federated Provinces shall be considered as consisting of three divisions: 1st—Upper Canada; 2nd—Lower Canada; 3rd—Nova Scotia, New Brunswick and Prince Edward Island; each division with an equal representation in the Legislative Council.

8. Upper Canada shall be represented in the Legislative Council by 24 Members, Lower Canada by 24 Members, and the three Maritime Provinces by 24 Members, of which Nova Scotia shall have ten, and New Brunswick ten, and Prince Edward Island four Members.

9. The Colony of Newfoundland shall be entitled to enter the proposed Union with a representation in the Legislative Council of four members.

10. The North-West Territory, British Columbia, and Vancouver, shall be admitted into the Union on such terms and conditions as the Parliament of the Federated Provinces shall deem equitable, and as shall receive the assent of Her Majesty; and in the case of the Province of British Columbia or Vancouver, as shall be agreed to by the Legislature of such Province.

11. The Members of the Legislative Council shall be appointed by the Crown under the Great Seal of the General Government, and shall hold office during Life. If any Legislative Councillor shall, for two consecutive Sessions of Parliament, fail to give his attendance in the said Council, his seat shall thereby become vacant.

12. The Members of the Legislative Council shall be British Subjects by Birth or Naturalization, of the full age of Thirty Years; shall possess a continuous real property qualification of four thousand dollars over and above all incumbrances, and shall be and continue worth that sum over and above their debts and liabilities; but in the case of Newfoundland and Prince Edward Island the property may be either real or personal.

13. If any question shall arise as to the qualification of a Legislative Councillor, the same shall be determined by the Council.

14. The first selection of the Members of the Legislative Council shall be made, except as regards Prince Edward Island, from the Legislative Councils of the various Provinces, so far as a sufficient number be found qualified and willing to serve; such

PRICELESS SOUVENIRS

Étienne-Paschal Taché, Premier of the Province of Canada since the spring of 1864, presided over the Quebec Conference a few months later. The inkstand seen in front of him in the photograph of Conference delegates was presented to him as a token of respect at the end of the meeting. Given to the Canadian people by one of Taché's descendants, the inkstand would be pressed into service again during the Quebec Conference of 1943, as well as for the signing of the Terms of Union by which Newfoundland joined Confederation in 1949.

A few other relics of the Quebec Conference exist today. The descendants of Jean-Charles Chapais, one of the Fathers of Confederation, carefully preserved the armchair which he reportedly occupied during the conference. A table said to have been used by the delegates was moved with the furniture of the Parliamentary offices in Québec City to those in Ottawa in 1865. There it was used by the Privy Council for two decades, before being passed on to the governments of Manitoba and the Northwest Territories. Over the years, this table was shortened and placed in the Legislative Assembly of the young province of Saskatchewan, in Regina.

Inkstand presented to Étienne-Paschal Taché in 1864.

Delegates to the Quebec Conference, 1864.
Photograph by Jules I. Livernois.

LIVELY DEBATE

At the end of the Quebec Conference, 72 resolutions, amounting to a draft constitution, were adopted. Delegates were tasked with presenting these resolutions to the Legislative Assemblies of their respective colonies and obtaining their ratification. This was easier said than done. Confederation was hotly debated in the legislatures and in newspapers. In Nova Scotia, Joseph Howe famously expressed his opposition to the union initiative in a series of open letters titled "The Botheration Scheme." While Canada, Nova Scotia and New Brunswick ratified the resolutions, Prince Edward Island held out.

La Scie, December 2, 1864.

LA CONFEDERATION!!!

In the pages of the newspaper *La Scie*, pioneering Canadian political cartoonist Jean-Baptiste Côté depicted the dubious "Effect of Confederation." Elsewhere in the same issue, he depicted the Confederation project as a "fearsome Gorgon" who, ridden by George Brown, threatens Lower Canada, represented here as a sheep. Two French Canadians wave incense to ward off the evil.

LONDON: THE HOME STRETCH

A third conference began in London on December 4, 1866. Ratified by the Legislative Assemblies of three of the North American colonies, the resolutions from the Quebec Conference now needed to be revised and validated by the imperial government.

A bill called the *British North America Act* — essentially a constitution — was introduced in both Houses of British Parliament, and was approved. As the name of the new country had not yet been settled by the end of January 1867, it was simply referred to as "the United Colony." It was not until the final draft, at the beginning of February, that the name "Canada" would appear to describe the new country, along with the new provincial designations of "Ontario" and "Quebec."

The Westminster Palace Hotel, where the delegates stayed and where several sessions of the London Conference were held.

Engraving by J. M. Williams, from the *London Illustrated News*, February 25, 1860.

CUTTING A FINE FIGURE

Queen Victoria finally received the delegates at Court and, on March 29, 1867, gave royal assent to Confederation.

As representatives of the governments of their respective colonies, most of the delegates were expected to wear a military-style uniform on special occasions. This coat, cocked hat, and buckles belonged to John A. Macdonald, George-Étienne Cartier and Alexander Galt, respectively. They were likely worn during encounters with Queen Victoria in 1867. Matching trousers or breeches completed the ensemble. Between work sessions and official meetings, the men made frequent visits to their tailors to ensure that they cut a fine figure.

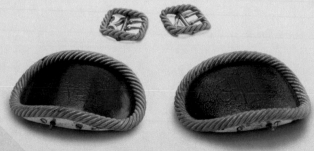

Cocked hat belonging to
George-Étienne Cartier,
around 1859–1870.

Coat belonging to Sir John A.
Macdonald, around 1859–1866.

Buckles for shoes and
breeches belonging to
Alexander Tilloch Galt.

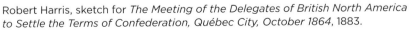
Robert Harris, sketch for *The Meeting of the Delegates of British North America to Settle the Terms of Confederation, Québec City, October 1864*, 1883.

THE FATHERS OF CONFEDERATION: AN ICONIC IMAGE

The 36 delegates present at the Charlottetown, Quebec and London Conferences would eventually become known as the "Fathers of Confederation." They represented not only the governments in power in each colony, but also the official oppositions. Most were lawyers and businessmen, publishers and journalists, but the group also included a pharmacist, a shipbuilder and a brewer. Some of them had been born in England and Scotland, but most were native to the colonies.

Depicting the Quebec Conference, this charcoal and sanguine sketch on vellum (pages 100–101) served as the preparatory drawing for the most famous portrayal of the Fathers of Confederation. This commemorative work was commissioned from artist Robert Harris by the Canadian government in 1883, nearly two decades after the event. The resulting oil painting was hung in the Centre Block of the Parliament buildings in Ottawa and was widely reproduced. Destroyed in the 1916 fire, the painting by Harris was recreated by artist Rex Woods for Canada's centennial in 1967.

THE *BRITISH NORTH AMERICA ACT*

The *British North America Act*, drafted by colonial delegates and given assent by the British Parliament and the Queen, became the new country's constitution. Unlike previous constitutions, which had been imposed by the government of Great Britain, this document's content had been developed by the colonies' own political representatives. But because it is an Act of the British Parliament, the original text is still kept in London.

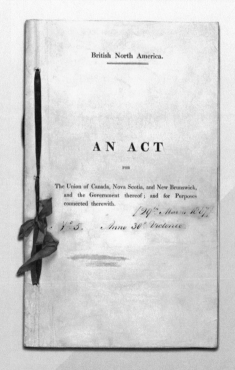

A NEW
STATE

JULY 1, 1867 — CONFEDERATION

On July 1, 1867 the *British North America Act* came into effect, marking the birth of the Dominion of Canada. The new nation included four provinces: Nova Scotia, New Brunswick, Quebec and Ontario. The legislative assemblies of the provinces now shared power with a federal parliament headquartered in Ottawa. The latter had two houses: the House of Commons, where elected members sat and the party with a majority formed the government; and the Senate, whose members were appointed. For the former colonies of British North America, this was a new beginning.

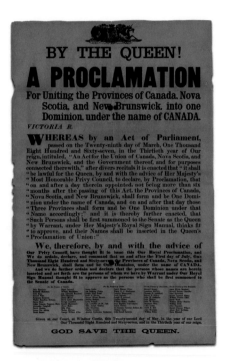

Broadside proclaiming Confederation, 1867.

Population: 1,160,000
65 | 24

Population: 270,000
15 | 12

Population: 1,500,000
82 | 24

Population: 350,000
19 | 12

Newfoundland

St. John's

Prince Edward Island

Charlottetown
Nova Scotia

QUEBEC

New Brunswick

Québec

Fredericton

Halifax

OTTAWA

ONTARIO

Toronto

★ Federal capital

⊛ Provincial capital

Number of seats in the federal Parliament

● House of Commons
● Senate

A TIME FOR CELEBRATION

Monday, July 1, 1867 was a holiday across the new country. Shops were closed, and business was suspended for the day. The royal proclamation that announced Confederation was read out in public. The weather was perfect. Enthusiastic crowds strolled down streets decorated with flags and banners. People attended military parades and sporting events. In the evening, bonfires and fireworks lit up the night sky.

In towns and cities, garrisoned soldiers and militia units paraded and saluted the royal proclamation with volleys of muskets and artillery. In ports, warships did the same. Commanders reviewed their troops in front of large crowds, while brass bands played patriotic airs such as "God Save the Queen."

Hiking, games and athletic competitions were among the most popular activities on July 1, 1867. In Montréal, the highlight of the day was a lacrosse game between the Montreal Lacrosse Club and the team from the Mohawk reserve at Kahnawake, which won the match. The irony was undoubtedly lost on the spectators: although Aboriginal peoples found themselves at the heart of the celebrations, they had not been consulted during the constitutional negotiations, nor had their interests been taken into account.

Lacrosse team from Kahnawake.
Photograph taken by William Notman in Montréal in 1867.

Surprisingly few photographs exist of the events on July 1, 1867 — the first day of Confederation. This one, taken by Elihu Spencer, shows the crowd on Parliament Hill.

GRUMBLING IN THE MARITIMES

Enthusiasm was not universal. In Halifax, this historic occasion was marked with a funeral procession and the burning in effigy of provincial Premier Charles Tupper.

In the Maritimes, and especially in Nova Scotia, the "anti-Confederation" movement would remain strong for a number of years. It was hoped that the *British North America Act* would be repealed, as Confederation was seen as an infringement of the very principle of responsible government.

It seemed that the powers taken away from the government in London twenty years before were now being surrendered to the government in Ottawa. The threat of new taxes also made merchants nervous. Feeling betrayed by their political leaders, people expressed their anger at the ballot box and caused the fall, in the autumn of 1867, of the government of Tupper, who had supported Confederation.

THREE CHEERS FOR THE "ANTIES"!

This banner was carried in 1867 by nine-year-old Robert Dawson, Jr. during an anti-Confederation procession in Bridgewater, Nova Scotia.

Robert was the son of a businessman who was well known in his community, and would one day become a prominent citizen himself.

OTTAWA, THE CAPITAL

In 1857, Queen Victoria had chosen Ottawa as the capital of the Province of Canada. By selecting this small town on the border between Canada West and Canada East, she hoped to settle the dispute between Montréal, Toronto, Québec City and Kingston, all of which had been vying for the honour. Construction of the buildings that would ultimately house the new federal Parliament began in 1859.

Very little remains from the centre block of Parliament that existed in 1867, as it was destroyed by fire in 1916.

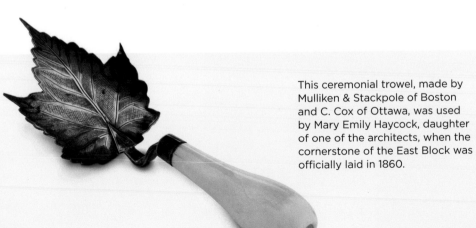

This ceremonial trowel, made by Mulliken & Stackpole of Boston and C. Cox of Ottawa, was used by Mary Emily Haycock, daughter of one of the architects, when the cornerstone of the East Block was officially laid in 1860.

PRIME MINISTER MACDONALD

John A. Macdonald was officially appointed by the Governor General, Lord Monck, to form the first cabinet under Confederation. For this first Cabinet, Macdonald surrounded himself with long-time associates, including George-Étienne Cartier and Alexander Galt. On July 5, 1867, his wife Agnes recorded in her diary that, even at home, "the atmosphere is so awfully political — that sometimes I think the very flies hold Parliaments on the Kitchen Table cloths!"

Document case belonging to George-Étienne Cartier, and pocket watch, made around 1780–1830, belonging to John A. Macdonald.

SHARED AUTHORITY

The principle of responsible government dictates that the Speech from the Throne — which opens each session of Parliament and lays out the government's priorities — be delivered by the Governor General, but written by the Prime Minister's Office. It was likely John A. Macdonald himself who composed the very first Speech from the Throne, which was given by Lord Monck on November 7, 1867.

It was from this imposing armchair (left), adorned with rococo motifs, armrests with lion's heads, and the monogram "VR" for "Victoria Regina" (Queen Victoria), that Lord Monck delivered the first Speech from the Throne.

Before being placed in the Senate in Ottawa, it had served Governors General in the Legislative Council of Québec City (1851–1865) since the time of Lord Elgin. It remained in the Senate until 1877.

This relatively simple walnut chair (right) was made in the studio of William Drum for the Legislative Assembly of the Province of Canada in 1863. Moved to Ottawa in 1866, it was used by the first Speaker of the House of Commons, the Honourable James Cockburn, from 1867 to 1873. At the time, Speakers of the House were each given their own chair and were allowed to keep it at the end of their term. Cockburn's descendants graciously presented this one to the House of Commons in 1983.

SYMBOLS AND SOUVENIRS

As a new nation, Canada needed a Great Seal, which would be affixed to official documents issued by the government in the name of the sovereign. The brothers Joseph Shepherd Wyon and Alfred Benjamin Wyon, London engravers, were commissioned to produce the seal, which was finally delivered to the Governor General in 1869. In the interim, the Great Seal of the Province of Canada was used. The new Great Seal, bearing the image of Queen Victoria, was used until it was replaced in turn with a seal bearing the image of Edward VII, in 1904.

The Canadian government also commissioned the Wyon brothers to design a commemorative medal. Struck in silver and bronze, these medals were distributed to the politicians and dignitaries involved in the Confederation initiative. A one-of-a-kind gold version was presented to Queen Victoria herself. The Latin inscription, "*Juventas Et Patrius Vigor Canada Instaurata 1867*" (Youth and patriotic strength, Canada inaugurated, 1867) attests to the spirit of the moment.

Opening of the first Parliament of the new Dominion, November 7, 1867.

Confederation
Medal in silver,
1867.

Great Seal of Canada, 1869.

A NATION IN THE MAKING

Canada became a nation in 1867, but the work of Confederation would continue for years to come. The new country — which would one day stretch from sea to sea — had only four provinces. It enjoyed greater autonomy in relation to Great Britain, but was by no means fully independent. Its people would long remain British subjects, before becoming Canadian citizens in their own right. Over the course of the 20th century, they would only gradually gain the democratic rights, symbols, and values that we take for granted today.

"Within your own borders peace, security and prosperity prevail, and I fervently pray that... you may be endowed with such a spirit of moderation and wisdom as will cause you to render the great work of Union which has been achieved, a blessing to yourselves and your posterity, and a fresh starting point in the moral, political and material advancement of the people of Canada."

Lord Monck, Governor General, first Speech from the Throne, November 7, 1867

CONTRIBUTIONS

I would like to thank all members of the exhibition's core team — whose composition evolved considerably during this project — for their creative input, including Dominique Savard, Chantal Brulé, Stéphane Breton, Dave Deevey, Jennifer Anderson, Brigitte Beaulne-Syp, Sophie Doucet and Danielle Goyer. Other colleagues at the Museum provided helpful advice: particularly Xavier Gélinas, Timothy Foran and Forrest Pass. Aaron Boyes, Geordie Wills, Anaïs Biernat, and above all, Alison Ward, provided essential research assistance. This souvenir catalogue owes its production to Publications Coordinator Lee Wyndham, and to photographer Steven Darby.

Finally, I would like to acknowledge the invaluable contributions of individuals and institutions who generously loaned artifacts from their collections and allowed reproduction rights for the images that have enriched both the content of the exhibition and this catalogue.

PHOTO CREDITS

© Canadian Museum of History

External Copyright